Keep the Vision

A 90-Day Planner

&

Daily Goal Setting Journal

Welcome Letter

Core Areas of Attention Pages

A One Year Timeline at a Glance Pages

Blank Monthly Calendars

My Daily Plan Pages

Morning & Evening Reflection Pages

A 90-Day Review

Notes

Keep the Vision

*

A 90-Day Planner

&

Daily Goal Setting Journal

Copyright © 2021,2022 by Nely Sanchez

ALL RIGHTS RESERVED

No part of this book may be reproduced, scanned, or transmitted in any form, or by any means whatsoever (electronic, mechanical, or otherwise) including photocopying, without the prior written permission and consent of the publisher, except where permitted by law.

Hardcover (Pink):   ISBN 13: 978-1-951137-02-1
Paperback (Pink):   ISBN 13: 978-1-951137-03-8
*
Hardcover (Black): ISBN 13: 978-1-951137-06-9
Paperback (Black): ISBN 13: 978-1-951137-08-3
*
Hardcover (Teal):   ISBN 13: 978-1-951137-10-6
Paperback (Teal):   ISBN 13: 978-1-951137-12-0

BCLS Creative Publishing Group

Welcome to your *Keep the Vision* planner!

Our sincere hope is that this planner will be a special place for you to jot down your short and long-term vision goals for your life, along with the plan to bring those goals to fruition.

Your dreams are important. Visualize them. Pray about them. Think about the steps you need to take in order to accomplish them.

Then get your ideas out of your head and down on paper.

Begin with the **Core Areas of Attention** pages by writing your short and long-term vision goals. Write the plan or action steps needed to accomplish these goals. Also, write down why a goal is important to you and how this dream could change your life for the better.

The **One Year Timeline at a Glance** pages can help you to quickly see the important events and deadlines for the current year and the next, and what you hope to accomplish each month.

On the **Blank Monthly Calendars**, jot down any appointments, deadlines, family events, etc., to help you better stay on track.

On the **My Daily Plan** pages, write down your schedule for the day, your to-do list, and your meal and exercise plans.

The **Morning & Evening Reflection** pages are where you can write your inspirational quote or memory verse, your gratitude list, and your goal setting actions for the day.

Write your *Top Life Goals* and your *Top 90-Day Goals* from your **Core Areas of Attention** pages during your morning reflection time. It's important to write your goals down every day to keep them front and center in your life.

During your evening reflection time, write down your accomplishments for the day and the things you might need to improve on tomorrow. Journal about the events of your day to record your progress, put things into perspective, and to clear your mind.

Concentrate on 90-day cycles, and work efficiently in that time frame in order to reach your dreams. There is a **90-Day Review** section at the end of this planner to examine your progress.

More importantly, step out in faith! Don't give up on your dreams. No matter where you are in your life, or where you've been.

Just keep moving forward with your plans and course-correct where and when needed.

As Always,

Keep the Vision!

★

Now let's begin!

Core Areas of Attention

In each box, write down <u>one</u> core area of attention that you want to work on in your life. Ex: Fitness, Marriage, Career, Change of Habit. Beneath your core area of attention, expand on this goal and write down the actionable steps you need to take in order to accomplish it. Review your goals daily. *Revise* and *Update* at least every 90 days to stay on track.
Write your Top Life Goals and Top 90-Day Goals on your *Morning & Evening Reflection* pages every day.

Core Area of Attention:_____

Action Steps:

This Goal Is Important To Me Because:

Core Area of Attention:_____

Action Steps:

This Goal Is Important To Me Because:

Core Area of Attention:_____

Action Steps:

This Goal Is Important To Me Because:

Core Areas of Attention

In each box, write down <u>one</u> core area of attention that you want to work on in your life.
Ex: Fitness, Marriage, Career, Change of Habit. Beneath your core area of attention, expand on this goal and write down the actionable steps you need to take in order to accomplish it. Review your goals daily.
Revise and *Update* at least every 90 days to stay on track.
Write your Top Life Goals and Top 90-Day Goals on your *Morning & Evening Reflection* pages every day.

Core Area of Attention:_____
Action Steps:

This Goal Is Important To Me Because:

_____
Core Area of Attention:_____
Action Steps:

This Goal Is Important To Me Because:

_____
Core Area of Attention:_____
Action Steps:

This Goal Is Important To Me Because:

Core Areas of Attention

In each box, write down <u>one</u> core area of attention that you want to work on in your life. Ex: Fitness, Marriage, Career, Change of Habit. Beneath your core area of attention, expand on this goal and write down the actionable steps you need to take in order to accomplish it. Review your goals daily. *Revise* and *Update* at least every 90 days to stay on track.

Write your Top Life Goals and Top 90-Day Goals on your *Morning & Evening Reflection* pages every day.

Core Area of Attention:_____
Action Steps:

This Goal Is Important To Me Because:

Core Area of Attention:_____
Action Steps:

This Goal Is Important To Me Because:

Core Area of Attention:_____
Action Steps:

This Goal Is Important To Me Because:

Core Areas of Attention

In each box, write down <u>one</u> core area of attention that you want to work on in your life. Ex: Fitness, Marriage, Career, Change of Habit. Beneath your core area of attention, expand on this goal and write down the actionable steps you need to take in order to accomplish it. Review your goals daily. *Revise* and *Update* at least every 90 days to stay on track.
Write your Top Life Goals and Top 90-Day Goals on your *Morning & Evening Reflection* pages every day.

Core Area of Attention: _____
Action Steps:

This Goal Is Important To Me Because:

_____

Core Area of Attention: _____
Action Steps:

This Goal Is Important To Me Because:

_____

Core Area of Attention: _____
Action Steps:

This Goal Is Important To Me Because:

Core Areas of Attention

In each box, write down <u>one</u> core area of attention that you want to work on in your life. Ex: Fitness, Marriage, Career, Change of Habit. Beneath your core area of attention, expand on this goal and write down the actionable steps you need to take in order to accomplish it. Review your goals daily. *Revise* and *Update* at least every 90 days to stay on track.
Write your Top Life Goals and Top 90-Day Goals on your *Morning & Evening Reflection* pages every day.

Core Area of Attention:_____
Action Steps:

This Goal Is Important To Me Because:

Core Area of Attention:_____
Action Steps:

This Goal Is Important To Me Because:

Core Area of Attention:_____
Action Steps:

This Goal Is Important To Me Because:

Core Areas of Attention

In each box, write down <u>one</u> core area of attention that you want to work on in your life. Ex: Fitness, Marriage, Career, Change of Habit. Beneath your core area of attention, expand on this goal and write down the actionable steps you need to take in order to accomplish it. Review your goals daily. *Revise* and *Update* at least every 90 days to stay on track.

Write your Top Life Goals and Top 90-Day Goals on your *Morning & Evening Reflection* pages every day.

Core Area of Attention: _____

Action Steps:

This Goal Is Important To Me Because:

_____

Core Area of Attention: _____

Action Steps:

This Goal Is Important To Me Because:

_____

Core Area of Attention: _____

Action Steps:

This Goal Is Important To Me Because:

Core Areas of Attention

In each box, write down <u>one</u> core area of attention that you want to work on in your life.
Ex: Fitness, Marriage, Career, Change of Habit. Beneath your core area of attention, expand on this goal and write down the actionable steps you need to take in order to accomplish it. Review your goals daily.
Revise and *Update* at least every 90 days to stay on track.
Write your Top Life Goals and Top 90-Day Goals on your *Morning & Evening Reflection* pages every day.

Core Area of Attention: _____

Action Steps:

This Goal Is Important To Me Because:

Core Area of Attention: _____

Action Steps:

This Goal Is Important To Me Because:

Core Area of Attention: _____

Action Steps:

This Goal Is Important To Me Because:

A One Year Timeline at a Glance

Write down important dates, goal deadlines, travel plans, etc.
Review this calendar daily and take actionable steps to stay on track.
Revise and *Update* as needed.
Year:_____

January	February	March

April	May	June

July	August	September

October	November	December

A One Year Timeline at a Glance

Write down important dates, goal deadlines, travel plans, etc.
Review this calendar daily and take actionable steps to stay on track.
Revise and *Update* as needed.
Year:_____

January	February	March

April	May	June

July	August	September

October	November	December

MONTH:

Sunday	Monday	Tuesday	Wednesday	Thursday	Friday	Saturday
—	—	—	—	—	—	—
—	—	—	—	—	—	—
—	—	—	—	—	—	—
—	—	—	—	—	—	—
—	—	—	—	—	—	—
—	—	—	—	—	—	—

MONTH:

Sunday	Monday	Tuesday	Wednesday	Thursday	Friday	Saturday
___	___	___	___	___	___	___
___	___	___	___	___	___	___
___	___	___	___	___	___	___
___	___	___	___	___	___	___
___	___	___	___	___	___	___
___	___	___	___	___	___	___

MONTH:

Sunday	Monday	Tuesday	Wednesday	Thursday	Friday	Saturday
—	—	—	—	—	—	—
—	—	—	—	—	—	—
—	—	—	—	—	—	—
—	—	—	—	—	—	—
—	—	—	—	—	—	—
—	—	—	—	—	—	—

MONTH:

Sunday	Monday	Tuesday	Wednesday	Thursday	Friday	Saturday
—	—	—	—	—	—	—
—	—	—	—	—	—	—
—	—	—	—	—	—	—
—	—	—	—	—	—	—
—	—	—	—	—	—	—
—	—	—	—	—	—	—

Notes

Notes

My Daily Plan

Date:_____

To-Do

Meal Plan

Breakfast:

Lunch:

Dinner:

Snacks:

Exercise & Water

Workout:

Water Goal:

Actual:

Notes

Schedule

5am_____
6am_____
7am_____
8am_____
9am_____
10am_____
11am_____
12pm_____
1pm_____
2pm_____
3pm_____
4pm_____
5pm_____
6pm_____
7pm_____
8pm_____

Other

Morning & Evening Reflection

Inspirational Quote / Memory Verse

What I'm Grateful For Today

Top Life Goals

Top 90-Day Goals

Goal Setting Actions for Today

My Accomplishments of the Day

What I Need To Improve On Tomorrow

Journal of My Day

_____
_____
_____
_____
_____
_____
_____
_____
_____
_____

My Daily Plan

Date:_____

To-Do

Meal Plan

Breakfast:

Lunch:

Dinner:

Snacks:

Exercise & Water

Workout:

Water Goal:

Actual:

Notes

Schedule

5am_____
6am_____
7am_____
8am_____
9am_____
10am_____
11am_____
12pm_____
1pm_____
2pm_____
3pm_____
4pm_____
5pm_____
6pm_____
7pm_____
8pm_____

Other

Morning & Evening Reflection

Inspirational Quote / Memory Verse

What I'm Grateful For Today

Top Life Goals

Top 90-Day Goals

Goal Setting Actions for Today

My Accomplishments of the Day

What I Need To Improve On Tomorrow

Journal of My Day

_____
_____
_____
_____
_____
_____
_____
_____
_____
_____

My Daily Plan

Date:_____

To-Do

Meal Plan

Breakfast:

Lunch:

Dinner:

Snacks:

Exercise & Water

Workout:

Water Goal:

Actual:

Notes

Schedule

5am_____
6am_____
7am_____
8am_____
9am_____
10am_____
11am_____
12pm_____
1pm_____
2pm_____
3pm_____
4pm_____
5pm_____
6pm_____
7pm_____
8pm_____

Other

Morning & Evening Reflection

Inspirational Quote / Memory Verse

What I'm Grateful For Today

Top Life Goals

Top 90-Day Goals

Goal Setting Actions for Today

My Accomplishments of the Day

What I Need To Improve On Tomorrow

Journal of My Day

_____
_____
_____
_____
_____
_____
_____
_____
_____
_____

My Daily Plan

Date:_____

To-Do

Meal Plan

Breakfast:

Lunch:

Dinner:

Snacks:

Exercise & Water

Workout:

Water Goal:

Actual:

Notes

Schedule

5am_____
6am_____
7am_____
8am_____
9am_____
10am_____
11am_____
12pm_____
1pm_____
2pm_____
3pm_____
4pm_____
5pm_____
6pm_____
7pm_____
8pm_____

Other

Morning & Evening Reflection

Inspirational Quote / Memory Verse

What I'm Grateful For Today

Top Life Goals

Top 90-Day Goals

Goal Setting Actions for Today

My Accomplishments of the Day

What I Need To Improve On Tomorrow

Journal of My Day

_____
_____
_____
_____
_____
_____
_____
_____
_____
_____

My Daily Plan

Date:_____

To-Do

Meal Plan

Breakfast:

Lunch:

Dinner:

Snacks:

Exercise & Water

Workout:

Water Goal:

Actual:

Notes

Schedule

5am_____
6am_____
7am_____
8am_____
9am_____
10am_____
11am_____
12pm_____
1pm_____
2pm_____
3pm_____
4pm_____
5pm_____
6pm_____
7pm_____
8pm_____

Other

Morning & Evening Reflection

Inspirational Quote / Memory Verse

What I'm Grateful For Today

Top Life Goals

Top 90-Day Goals

Goal Setting Actions for Today

My Accomplishments of the Day

What I Need To Improve On Tomorrow

Journal of My Day

_____
_____
_____
_____
_____
_____
_____
_____
_____

My Daily Plan

Date:_____

To-Do

Meal Plan

Breakfast:

Lunch:

Dinner:

Snacks:

Exercise & Water

Workout:

Water Goal:

Actual:

Notes

Schedule

5am_____
6am_____
7am_____
8am_____
9am_____
10am_____
11am_____
12pm_____
1pm_____
2pm_____
3pm_____
4pm_____
5pm_____
6pm_____
7pm_____
8pm_____

Other

Morning & Evening Reflection

Inspirational Quote / Memory Verse

What I'm Grateful For Today

Top Life Goals

Top 90-Day Goals

Goal Setting Actions for Today

My Accomplishments of the Day

What I Need To Improve On Tomorrow

Journal of My Day

_____
_____
_____
_____
_____
_____
_____
_____
_____
_____

My Daily Plan

Date:_____

To-Do

Meal Plan

Breakfast:

Lunch:

Dinner:

Snacks:

Exercise & Water

Workout:

Water Goal:

Actual:

Notes

Schedule

5am_____
6am_____
7am_____
8am_____
9am_____
10am_____
11am_____
12pm_____
1pm_____
2pm_____
3pm_____
4pm_____
5pm_____
6pm_____
7pm_____
8pm_____

Other

Morning & Evening Reflection

Inspirational Quote / Memory Verse

What I'm Grateful For Today

Top Life Goals

Top 90-Day Goals

Goal Setting Actions for Today

My Accomplishments of the Day

What I Need To Improve On Tomorrow

Journal of My Day

_____
_____
_____
_____
_____
_____
_____
_____
_____
_____

My Daily Plan

Date:_____

To-Do

Meal Plan

Breakfast:

Lunch:

Dinner:

Snacks:

Exercise & Water

Workout:

Water Goal:

Actual:

Notes

Schedule

5am_____
6am_____
7am_____
8am_____
9am_____
10am_____
11am_____
12pm_____
1pm_____
2pm_____
3pm_____
4pm_____
5pm_____
6pm_____
7pm_____
8pm_____

Other

Morning & Evening Reflection

Inspirational Quote / Memory Verse

What I'm Grateful For Today

Top Life Goals

Top 90-Day Goals

Goal Setting Actions for Today

My Accomplishments of the Day

What I Need To Improve On Tomorrow

Journal of My Day

_____
_____
_____
_____
_____
_____
_____
_____
_____
_____

My Daily Plan

Date:_____

To-Do

Meal Plan

Breakfast:

Lunch:

Dinner:

Snacks:

Exercise & Water

Workout:

Water Goal:

Actual:

Notes

Schedule

5am_____
6am_____
7am_____
8am_____
9am_____
10am_____
11am_____
12pm_____
1pm_____
2pm_____
3pm_____
4pm_____
5pm_____
6pm_____
7pm_____
8pm_____

Other

Morning & Evening Reflection

Inspirational Quote / Memory Verse

What I'm Grateful For Today

Top Life Goals

Top 90-Day Goals

Goal Setting Actions for Today

My Accomplishments of the Day

What I Need To Improve On Tomorrow

Journal of My Day

_____
_____
_____
_____
_____
_____
_____
_____
_____
_____

My Daily Plan

Date:_____

To-Do

Meal Plan

Breakfast:

Lunch:

Dinner:

Snacks:

Exercise & Water

Workout:

Water Goal:

Actual:

Notes

Schedule

5am_____
6am_____
7am_____
8am_____
9am_____
10am_____
11am_____
12pm_____
1pm_____
2pm_____
3pm_____
4pm_____
5pm_____
6pm_____
7pm_____
8pm_____

Other

Morning & Evening Reflection

Inspirational Quote / Memory Verse

What I'm Grateful For Today

Top Life Goals

Top 90-Day Goals

Goal Setting Actions for Today

My Accomplishments of the Day

What I Need To Improve On Tomorrow

Journal of My Day

_____
_____
_____
_____
_____
_____
_____
_____
_____
_____
_____
_____

My Daily Plan

Date:_____

To-Do

Meal Plan

Breakfast:

Lunch:

Dinner:

Snacks:

Exercise & Water

Workout:

Water Goal:

Actual:

Notes

Schedule

5am_____
6am_____
7am_____
8am_____
9am_____
10am_____
11am_____
12pm_____
1pm_____
2pm_____
3pm_____
4pm_____
5pm_____
6pm_____
7pm_____
8pm_____

Other

Morning & Evening Reflection

Inspirational Quote / Memory Verse

What I'm Grateful For Today

Top Life Goals

Top 90-Day Goals

Goal Setting Actions for Today

My Accomplishments of the Day

What I Need To Improve On Tomorrow

Journal of My Day

_____
_____
_____
_____
_____
_____
_____
_____
_____
_____

My Daily Plan

Date:_____

To-Do

Meal Plan

Breakfast:

Lunch:

Dinner:

Snacks:

Exercise & Water

Workout:

Water Goal:

Actual:

Notes

Schedule

5am_____
6am_____
7am_____
8am_____
9am_____
10am_____
11am_____
12pm_____
1pm_____
2pm_____
3pm_____
4pm_____
5pm_____
6pm_____
7pm_____
8pm_____

Other

Morning & Evening Reflection

Inspirational Quote / Memory Verse

What I'm Grateful For Today

Top Life Goals

Top 90-Day Goals

Goal Setting Actions for Today

My Accomplishments of the Day

What I Need To Improve On Tomorrow

Journal of My Day

_____
_____
_____
_____
_____
_____
_____
_____
_____
_____
_____

My Daily Plan

Date:_____

To-Do

Meal Plan

Breakfast:

Lunch:

Dinner:

Snacks:

Exercise & Water

Workout:

Water Goal:

Actual:

Notes

Schedule

5am_____
6am_____
7am_____
8am_____
9am_____
10am_____
11am_____
12pm_____
1pm_____
2pm_____
3pm_____
4pm_____
5pm_____
6pm_____
7pm_____
8pm_____

Other

Morning & Evening Reflection

Inspirational Quote / Memory Verse

What I'm Grateful For Today

Top Life Goals

Top 90-Day Goals

Goal Setting Actions for Today

My Accomplishments of the Day

What I Need To Improve On Tomorrow

Journal of My Day

_____
_____
_____
_____
_____
_____
_____
_____
_____
_____

My Daily Plan

Date:_____

To-Do

Meal Plan

Breakfast:

Lunch:

Dinner:

Snacks:

Exercise & Water

Workout:

Water Goal:

Actual:

Notes

Schedule

5am_____
6am_____
7am_____
8am_____
9am_____
10am_____
11am_____
12pm_____
1pm_____
2pm_____
3pm_____
4pm_____
5pm_____
6pm_____
7pm_____
8pm_____

Other

Morning & Evening Reflection

Inspirational Quote / Memory Verse

What I'm Grateful For Today

Top Life Goals

Top 90-Day Goals

Goal Setting Actions for Today

My Accomplishments of the Day

What I Need To Improve On Tomorrow

Journal of My Day

_____
_____
_____
_____
_____
_____
_____
_____
_____

My Daily Plan

Date:_____

To-Do

Meal Plan

Breakfast:

Lunch:

Dinner:

Snacks:

Exercise & Water

Workout:

Water Goal:

Actual:

Notes

Schedule

5am_____
6am_____
7am_____
8am_____
9am_____
10am_____
11am_____
12pm_____
1pm_____
2pm_____
3pm_____
4pm_____
5pm_____
6pm_____
7pm_____
8pm_____

Other

Morning & Evening Reflection

Inspirational Quote / Memory Verse

What I'm Grateful For Today

Top Life Goals

Top 90-Day Goals

Goal Setting Actions for Today

My Accomplishments of the Day

What I Need To Improve On Tomorrow

Journal of My Day

_____
_____
_____
_____
_____
_____
_____
_____
_____
_____

My Daily Plan

Date:_____

To-Do

Meal Plan

Breakfast:

Lunch:

Dinner:

Snacks:

Exercise & Water

Workout:

Water Goal:

Actual:

Notes

Schedule

5am_____
6am_____
7am_____
8am_____
9am_____
10am_____
11am_____
12pm_____
1pm_____
2pm_____
3pm_____
4pm_____
5pm_____
6pm_____
7pm_____
8pm_____

Other

Morning & Evening Reflection

Inspirational Quote / Memory Verse

What I'm Grateful For Today

Top Life Goals

Top 90-Day Goals

Goal Setting Actions for Today

My Accomplishments of the Day

What I Need To Improve On Tomorrow

Journal of My Day

_____
_____
_____
_____
_____
_____
_____
_____
_____
_____

My Daily Plan

Date:_____

To-Do

Meal Plan

Breakfast:

Lunch:

Dinner:

Snacks:

Exercise & Water

Workout:

Water Goal:

Actual:

Notes

Schedule

5am_____
6am_____
7am_____
8am_____
9am_____
10am_____
11am_____
12pm_____
1pm_____
2pm_____
3pm_____
4pm_____
5pm_____
6pm_____
7pm_____
8pm_____

Other

Morning & Evening Reflection

Inspirational Quote / Memory Verse

What I'm Grateful For Today

Top Life Goals

Top 90-Day Goals

Goal Setting Actions for Today

My Accomplishments of the Day

What I Need To Improve On Tomorrow

Journal of My Day

_____
_____
_____
_____
_____
_____
_____
_____
_____
_____

My Daily Plan

Date:_____

To-Do

Meal Plan

Breakfast:

Lunch:

Dinner:

Snacks:

Exercise & Water

Workout:

Water Goal:

Actual:

Notes

Schedule

5am_____
6am_____
7am_____
8am_____
9am_____
10am_____
11am_____
12pm_____
1pm_____
2pm_____
3pm_____
4pm_____
5pm_____
6pm_____
7pm_____
8pm_____

Other

Morning & Evening Reflection

Inspirational Quote / Memory Verse

What I'm Grateful For Today

Top Life Goals

Top 90-Day Goals

Goal Setting Actions for Today

My Accomplishments of the Day

What I Need To Improve On Tomorrow

Journal of My Day

_____
_____
_____
_____
_____
_____
_____
_____
_____
_____

My Daily Plan

Date:_____

To-Do

Meal Plan

Breakfast:

Lunch:

Dinner:

Snacks:

Exercise & Water

Workout:

Water Goal:

Actual:

Notes

Schedule

5am_____
6am_____
7am_____
8am_____
9am_____
10am_____
11am_____
12pm_____
1pm_____
2pm_____
3pm_____
4pm_____
5pm_____
6pm_____
7pm_____
8pm_____

Other

Morning & Evening Reflection

Inspirational Quote / Memory Verse

What I'm Grateful For Today

Top Life Goals

Top 90-Day Goals

Goal Setting Actions for Today

My Accomplishments of the Day

What I Need To Improve On Tomorrow

Journal of My Day

_____
_____
_____
_____
_____
_____
_____
_____
_____
_____

My Daily Plan

Date:_____

To-Do

Meal Plan

Breakfast:

Lunch:

Dinner:

Snacks:

Exercise & Water

Workout:

Water Goal:

Actual:

Notes

Schedule

5am_____
6am_____
7am_____
8am_____
9am_____
10am_____
11am_____
12pm_____
1pm_____
2pm_____
3pm_____
4pm_____
5pm_____
6pm_____
7pm_____
8pm_____

Other

Morning & Evening Reflection

Inspirational Quote / Memory Verse

What I'm Grateful For Today

Top Life Goals

Top 90-Day Goals

Goal Setting Actions for Today

My Accomplishments of the Day

What I Need To Improve On Tomorrow

Journal of My Day

_____
_____
_____
_____
_____
_____
_____
_____
_____
_____

My Daily Plan

Date:_____

To-Do

Meal Plan

Breakfast:

Lunch:

Dinner:

Snacks:

Exercise & Water

Workout:

Water Goal:

Actual:

Notes

Schedule

5am_____
6am_____
7am_____
8am_____
9am_____
10am_____
11am_____
12pm_____
1pm_____
2pm_____
3pm_____
4pm_____
5pm_____
6pm_____
7pm_____
8pm_____

Other

Morning & Evening Reflection

Inspirational Quote / Memory Verse

What I'm Grateful For Today

Top Life Goals

Top 90-Day Goals

Goal Setting Actions for Today

My Accomplishments of the Day

What I Need To Improve On Tomorrow

Journal of My Day

_____
_____
_____
_____
_____
_____
_____
_____
_____
_____

My Daily Plan

Date:_____

To-Do

Meal Plan

Breakfast:

Lunch:

Dinner:

Snacks:

Exercise & Water

Workout:

Water Goal:

Actual:

Notes

Schedule

5am_____
6am_____
7am_____
8am_____
9am_____
10am_____
11am_____
12pm_____
1pm_____
2pm_____
3pm_____
4pm_____
5pm_____
6pm_____
7pm_____
8pm_____

Other

Morning & Evening Reflection

Inspirational Quote / Memory Verse

What I'm Grateful For Today

Top Life Goals

Top 90-Day Goals

Goal Setting Actions for Today

My Accomplishments of the Day

What I Need To Improve On Tomorrow

Journal of My Day

_____
_____
_____
_____
_____
_____
_____
_____
_____
_____

My Daily Plan

Date:_____

To-Do

Meal Plan

Breakfast:

Lunch:

Dinner:

Snacks:

Exercise & Water

Workout:

Water Goal:

Actual:

Notes

Schedule

5am_____
6am_____
7am_____
8am_____
9am_____
10am_____
11am_____
12pm_____
1pm_____
2pm_____
3pm_____
4pm_____
5pm_____
6pm_____
7pm_____
8pm_____

Other

Morning & Evening Reflection

Inspirational Quote / Memory Verse

What I'm Grateful For Today

Top Life Goals

Top 90-Day Goals

Goal Setting Actions for Today

My Accomplishments of the Day

What I Need To Improve On Tomorrow

Journal of My Day

_____
_____
_____
_____
_____
_____
_____
_____
_____
_____

My Daily Plan

Date:_____

To-Do

Meal Plan

Breakfast:

Lunch:

Dinner:

Snacks:

Exercise & Water

Workout:

Water Goal:

Actual:

Notes

Schedule

5am_____
6am_____
7am_____
8am_____
9am_____
10am_____
11am_____
12pm_____
1pm_____
2pm_____
3pm_____
4pm_____
5pm_____
6pm_____
7pm_____
8pm_____

Other

Morning & Evening Reflection

Inspirational Quote / Memory Verse

What I'm Grateful For Today

Top Life Goals

Top 90-Day Goals

Goal Setting Actions for Today

My Accomplishments of the Day

What I Need To Improve On Tomorrow

Journal of My Day

_____
_____
_____
_____
_____
_____
_____
_____
_____
_____
_____

My Daily Plan

Date:_____

To-Do

Meal Plan

Breakfast:

Lunch:

Dinner:

Snacks:

Exercise & Water

Workout:

Water Goal:

Actual:

Notes

Schedule

5am_____
6am_____
7am_____
8am_____
9am_____
10am_____
11am_____
12pm_____
1pm_____
2pm_____
3pm_____
4pm_____
5pm_____
6pm_____
7pm_____
8pm_____

Other

Morning & Evening Reflection

Inspirational Quote / Memory Verse

What I'm Grateful For Today

Top Life Goals

Top 90-Day Goals

Goal Setting Actions for Today

My Accomplishments of the Day

What I Need To Improve On Tomorrow

Journal of My Day

_____
_____
_____
_____
_____
_____
_____
_____
_____
_____

My Daily Plan

Date:_____

To-Do

Meal Plan

Breakfast:

Lunch:

Dinner:

Snacks:

Exercise & Water

Workout:

Water Goal:

Actual:

Notes

Schedule

5am_____
6am_____
7am_____
8am_____
9am_____
10am_____
11am_____
12pm_____
1pm_____
2pm_____
3pm_____
4pm_____
5pm_____
6pm_____
7pm_____
8pm_____

Other

Morning & Evening Reflection

Inspirational Quote / Memory Verse

What I'm Grateful For Today

Top Life Goals

Top 90-Day Goals

Goal Setting Actions for Today

My Accomplishments of the Day

What I Need To Improve On Tomorrow

Journal of My Day

_____
_____
_____
_____
_____
_____
_____
_____
_____
_____

My Daily Plan

Date:_____

To-Do

Meal Plan

Breakfast:

Lunch:

Dinner:

Snacks:

Exercise & Water

Workout:

Water Goal:

Actual:

Notes

Schedule

5am_____
6am_____
7am_____
8am_____
9am_____
10am_____
11am_____
12pm_____
1pm_____
2pm_____
3pm_____
4pm_____
5pm_____
6pm_____
7pm_____
8pm_____

Other

Morning & Evening Reflection

Inspirational Quote / Memory Verse

What I'm Grateful For Today

Top Life Goals

Top 90-Day Goals

Goal Setting Actions for Today

My Accomplishments of the Day

What I Need To Improve On Tomorrow

Journal of My Day

_____
_____
_____
_____
_____
_____
_____
_____
_____
_____

My Daily Plan

Date:_____

To-Do

Meal Plan

Breakfast:

Lunch:

Dinner:

Snacks:

Exercise & Water

Workout:

Water Goal:

Actual:

Notes

Schedule

5am_____
6am_____
7am_____
8am_____
9am_____
10am_____
11am_____
12pm_____
1pm_____
2pm_____
3pm_____
4pm_____
5pm_____
6pm_____
7pm_____
8pm_____

Other

Morning & Evening Reflection

Inspirational Quote / Memory Verse

What I'm Grateful For Today

Top Life Goals

Top 90-Day Goals

Goal Setting Actions for Today

My Accomplishments of the Day

What I Need To Improve On Tomorrow

Journal of My Day

_____
_____
_____
_____
_____
_____
_____
_____
_____

My Daily Plan

Date:_____

To-Do

Meal Plan

Breakfast:

Lunch:

Dinner:

Snacks:

Exercise & Water

Workout:

Water Goal:

Actual:

Notes

Schedule

5am_____
6am_____
7am_____
8am_____
9am_____
10am_____
11am_____
12pm_____
1pm_____
2pm_____
3pm_____
4pm_____
5pm_____
6pm_____
7pm_____
8pm_____

Other

Morning & Evening Reflection

Inspirational Quote / Memory Verse

What I'm Grateful For Today

Top Life Goals

Top 90-Day Goals

Goal Setting Actions for Today

My Accomplishments of the Day

What I Need To Improve On Tomorrow

Journal of My Day

_____
_____
_____
_____
_____
_____
_____
_____
_____
_____
_____

My Daily Plan

Date:_____

To-Do

Meal Plan

Breakfast:

Lunch:

Dinner:

Snacks:

Exercise & Water

Workout:

Water Goal:

Actual:

Notes

Schedule

5am_____
6am_____
7am_____
8am_____
9am_____
10am_____
11am_____
12pm_____
1pm_____
2pm_____
3pm_____
4pm_____
5pm_____
6pm_____
7pm_____
8pm_____

Other

Morning & Evening Reflection

Inspirational Quote / Memory Verse

What I'm Grateful For Today

Top Life Goals

Top 90-Day Goals

Goal Setting Actions for Today

My Accomplishments of the Day

What I Need To Improve On Tomorrow

Journal of My Day

_____
_____
_____
_____
_____
_____
_____
_____
_____
_____

My Daily Plan

Date:_____

To-Do

Meal Plan

Breakfast:

Lunch:

Dinner:

Snacks:

Exercise & Water

Workout:

Water Goal:

Actual:

Notes

Schedule

5am_____
6am_____
7am_____
8am_____
9am_____
10am_____
11am_____
12pm_____
1pm_____
2pm_____
3pm_____
4pm_____
5pm_____
6pm_____
7pm_____
8pm_____

Other

Morning & Evening Reflection

Inspirational Quote / Memory Verse

What I'm Grateful For Today

Top Life Goals

Top 90-Day Goals

Goal Setting Actions for Today

My Accomplishments of the Day

What I Need To Improve On Tomorrow

Journal of My Day

_____
_____
_____
_____
_____
_____
_____
_____
_____
_____

My Daily Plan

Date:_____

To-Do

Meal Plan

Breakfast:

Lunch:

Dinner:

Snacks:

Exercise & Water

Workout:

Water Goal:

Actual:

Notes

Schedule

5am_____
6am_____
7am_____
8am_____
9am_____
10am_____
11am_____
12pm_____
1pm_____
2pm_____
3pm_____
4pm_____
5pm_____
6pm_____
7pm_____
8pm_____

Other

Morning & Evening Reflection

Inspirational Quote / Memory Verse

What I'm Grateful For Today

Top Life Goals

Top 90-Day Goals

Goal Setting Actions for Today

My Accomplishments of the Day

What I Need To Improve On Tomorrow

Journal of My Day

_____
_____
_____
_____
_____
_____
_____
_____
_____
_____

My Daily Plan

Date:_____

To-Do

Meal Plan

Breakfast:

Lunch:

Dinner:

Snacks:

Exercise & Water

Workout:

Water Goal:

Actual:

Notes

Schedule

5am_____
6am_____
7am_____
8am_____
9am_____
10am_____
11am_____
12pm_____
1pm_____
2pm_____
3pm_____
4pm_____
5pm_____
6pm_____
7pm_____
8pm_____

Other

Morning & Evening Reflection

Inspirational Quote / Memory Verse

What I'm Grateful For Today

Top Life Goals

Top 90-Day Goals

Goal Setting Actions for Today

My Accomplishments of the Day

What I Need To Improve On Tomorrow

Journal of My Day

_____
_____
_____
_____
_____
_____
_____
_____
_____
_____

My Daily Plan

Date:_____

To-Do

Meal Plan

Breakfast:

Lunch:

Dinner:

Snacks:

Exercise & Water

Workout:

Water Goal:

Actual:

Notes

Schedule

5am_____
6am_____
7am_____
8am_____
9am_____
10am_____
11am_____
12pm_____
1pm_____
2pm_____
3pm_____
4pm_____
5pm_____
6pm_____
7pm_____
8pm_____

Other

Morning & Evening Reflection

Inspirational Quote / Memory Verse

What I'm Grateful For Today

Top Life Goals

Top 90-Day Goals

Goal Setting Actions for Today

My Accomplishments of the Day

What I Need To Improve On Tomorrow

Journal of My Day

_____
_____
_____
_____
_____
_____
_____
_____
_____
_____

My Daily Plan

Date:_____

To-Do

Meal Plan

Breakfast:

Lunch:

Dinner:

Snacks:

Exercise & Water

Workout:

Water Goal:

Actual:

Notes

Schedule

5am_____
6am_____
7am_____
8am_____
9am_____
10am_____
11am_____
12pm_____
1pm_____
2pm_____
3pm_____
4pm_____
5pm_____
6pm_____
7pm_____
8pm_____

Other

Morning & Evening Reflection

Inspirational Quote / Memory Verse

What I'm Grateful For Today

Top Life Goals

Top 90-Day Goals

Goal Setting Actions for Today

My Accomplishments of the Day

What I Need To Improve On Tomorrow

Journal of My Day

_____
_____
_____
_____
_____
_____
_____
_____
_____
_____

My Daily Plan

Date:_____

To-Do

Meal Plan

Breakfast:

Lunch:

Dinner:

Snacks:

Exercise & Water

Workout:

Water Goal:

Actual:

Notes

Schedule

5am_____
6am_____
7am_____
8am_____
9am_____
10am_____
11am_____
12pm_____
1pm_____
2pm_____
3pm_____
4pm_____
5pm_____
6pm_____
7pm_____
8pm_____

Other

Morning & Evening Reflection

Inspirational Quote / Memory Verse   **What I'm Grateful For Today**

Top Life Goals   **Top 90-Day Goals**

Goal Setting Actions for Today

My Accomplishments of the Day   **What I Need To Improve On Tomorrow**

Journal of My Day

_____
_____
_____
_____
_____
_____
_____
_____
_____
_____

My Daily Plan

Date:_____

To-Do

Meal Plan

Breakfast:

Lunch:

Dinner:

Snacks:

Exercise & Water

Workout:

Water Goal:

Actual:

Notes

Schedule

5am_____
6am_____
7am_____
8am_____
9am_____
10am_____
11am_____
12pm_____
1pm_____
2pm_____
3pm_____
4pm_____
5pm_____
6pm_____
7pm_____
8pm_____

Other

Morning & Evening Reflection

Inspirational Quote / Memory Verse   **What I'm Grateful For Today**

Top Life Goals   **Top 90-Day Goals**

Goal Setting Actions for Today

My Accomplishments of the Day   **What I Need To Improve On Tomorrow**

Journal of My Day

_____
_____
_____
_____
_____
_____
_____
_____
_____
_____

My Daily Plan

Date:_____

To-Do

Meal Plan

Breakfast:

Lunch:

Dinner:

Snacks:

Exercise & Water

Workout:

Water Goal:

Actual:

Notes

Schedule

5am_____
6am_____
7am_____
8am_____
9am_____
10am_____
11am_____
12pm_____
1pm_____
2pm_____
3pm_____
4pm_____
5pm_____
6pm_____
7pm_____
8pm_____

Other

Morning & Evening Reflection

Inspirational Quote / Memory Verse

What I'm Grateful For Today

Top Life Goals

Top 90-Day Goals

Goal Setting Actions for Today

My Accomplishments of the Day

What I Need To Improve On Tomorrow

Journal of My Day

_____
_____
_____
_____
_____
_____
_____
_____
_____
_____
_____

My Daily Plan

Date:_____

To-Do

Meal Plan

Breakfast:

Lunch:

Dinner:

Snacks:

Exercise & Water

Workout:

Water Goal:

Actual:

Notes

Schedule

5am_____
6am_____
7am_____
8am_____
9am_____
10am_____
11am_____
12pm_____
1pm_____
2pm_____
3pm_____
4pm_____
5pm_____
6pm_____
7pm_____
8pm_____

Other

Morning & Evening Reflection

Inspirational Quote / Memory Verse

What I'm Grateful For Today

Top Life Goals

Top 90-Day Goals

Goal Setting Actions for Today

My Accomplishments of the Day

What I Need To Improve On Tomorrow

Journal of My Day

_____
_____
_____
_____
_____
_____
_____
_____
_____
_____

My Daily Plan

Date:_____

To-Do

Meal Plan

Breakfast:

Lunch:

Dinner:

Snacks:

Exercise & Water

Workout:

Water Goal:

Actual:

Notes

Schedule

5am_____
6am_____
7am_____
8am_____
9am_____
10am_____
11am_____
12pm_____
1pm_____
2pm_____
3pm_____
4pm_____
5pm_____
6pm_____
7pm_____
8pm_____

Other

Morning & Evening Reflection

Inspirational Quote / Memory Verse

What I'm Grateful For Today

Top Life Goals

Top 90-Day Goals

Goal Setting Actions for Today

My Accomplishments of the Day

What I Need To Improve On Tomorrow

Journal of My Day

_____
_____
_____
_____
_____
_____
_____
_____
_____
_____
_____

My Daily Plan

Date:_____

To-Do

Meal Plan

Breakfast:

Lunch:

Dinner:

Snacks:

Exercise & Water

Workout:

Water Goal:

Actual:

Notes

Schedule

5am_____
6am_____
7am_____
8am_____
9am_____
10am_____
11am_____
12pm_____
1pm_____
2pm_____
3pm_____
4pm_____
5pm_____
6pm_____
7pm_____
8pm_____

Other

Morning & Evening Reflection

Inspirational Quote / Memory Verse

What I'm Grateful For Today

Top Life Goals

Top 90-Day Goals

Goal Setting Actions for Today

My Accomplishments of the Day

What I Need To Improve On Tomorrow

Journal of My Day

_____
_____
_____
_____
_____
_____
_____
_____
_____
_____

My Daily Plan

Date:_____

To-Do

Meal Plan

Breakfast:

Lunch:

Dinner:

Snacks:

Exercise & Water

Workout:

Water Goal:

Actual:

Notes

Schedule

5am_____
6am_____
7am_____
8am_____
9am_____
10am_____
11am_____
12pm_____
1pm_____
2pm_____
3pm_____
4pm_____
5pm_____
6pm_____
7pm_____
8pm_____

Other

Morning & Evening Reflection

Inspirational Quote / Memory Verse

What I'm Grateful For Today

Top Life Goals

Top 90-Day Goals

Goal Setting Actions for Today

My Accomplishments of the Day

What I Need To Improve On Tomorrow

Journal of My Day

_____
_____
_____
_____
_____
_____
_____
_____
_____
_____

My Daily Plan

Date:_____

To-Do

Meal Plan

Breakfast:

Lunch:

Dinner:

Snacks:

Exercise & Water

Workout:

Water Goal:

Actual:

Notes

Schedule

5am_____
6am_____
7am_____
8am_____
9am_____
10am_____
11am_____
12pm_____
1pm_____
2pm_____
3pm_____
4pm_____
5pm_____
6pm_____
7pm_____
8pm_____

Other

Morning & Evening Reflection

Inspirational Quote / Memory Verse

What I'm Grateful For Today

Top Life Goals

Top 90-Day Goals

Goal Setting Actions for Today

My Accomplishments of the Day

What I Need To Improve On Tomorrow

Journal of My Day

_____
_____
_____
_____
_____
_____
_____
_____
_____
_____

My Daily Plan

Date:_____

To-Do

Meal Plan

Breakfast:

Lunch:

Dinner:

Snacks:

Exercise & Water

Workout:

Water Goal:

Actual:

Notes

Schedule

5am_____
6am_____
7am_____
8am_____
9am_____
10am_____
11am_____
12pm_____
1pm_____
2pm_____
3pm_____
4pm_____
5pm_____
6pm_____
7pm_____
8pm_____

Other

Morning & Evening Reflection

Inspirational Quote / Memory Verse

What I'm Grateful For Today

Top Life Goals

Top 90-Day Goals

Goal Setting Actions for Today

My Accomplishments of the Day

What I Need To Improve On Tomorrow

Journal of My Day

_____
_____
_____
_____
_____
_____
_____
_____
_____
_____

My Daily Plan

Date:_____

To-Do

Meal Plan

Breakfast:

Lunch:

Dinner:

Snacks:

Exercise & Water

Workout:

Water Goal:

Actual:

Notes

Schedule

5am_____
6am_____
7am_____
8am_____
9am_____
10am_____
11am_____
12pm_____
1pm_____
2pm_____
3pm_____
4pm_____
5pm_____
6pm_____
7pm_____
8pm_____

Other

Morning & Evening Reflection

Inspirational Quote / Memory Verse

What I'm Grateful For Today

Top Life Goals

Top 90-Day Goals

Goal Setting Actions for Today

My Accomplishments of the Day

What I Need To Improve On Tomorrow

Journal of My Day

_____
_____
_____
_____
_____
_____
_____
_____
_____
_____

My Daily Plan

Date:_____

To-Do

Meal Plan

Breakfast:

Lunch:

Dinner:

Snacks:

Exercise & Water

Workout:

Water Goal:

Actual:

Notes

Schedule

5am_____
6am_____
7am_____
8am_____
9am_____
10am_____
11am_____
12pm_____
1pm_____
2pm_____
3pm_____
4pm_____
5pm_____
6pm_____
7pm_____
8pm_____

Other

Morning & Evening Reflection

Inspirational Quote / Memory Verse

What I'm Grateful For Today

Top Life Goals

Top 90-Day Goals

Goal Setting Actions for Today

My Accomplishments of the Day

What I Need To Improve On Tomorrow

Journal of My Day

_____
_____
_____
_____
_____
_____
_____
_____
_____
_____

My Daily Plan

Date:_____

To-Do

Meal Plan

Breakfast:

Lunch:

Dinner:

Snacks:

Exercise & Water

Workout:

Water Goal:

Actual:

Notes

Schedule

5am_____
6am_____
7am_____
8am_____
9am_____
10am_____
11am_____
12pm_____
1pm_____
2pm_____
3pm_____
4pm_____
5pm_____
6pm_____
7pm_____
8pm_____

Other

Morning & Evening Reflection

Inspirational Quote / Memory Verse   **What I'm Grateful For Today**

Top Life Goals   **Top 90-Day Goals**

Goal Setting Actions for Today

My Accomplishments of the Day   **What I Need To Improve On Tomorrow**

Journal of My Day

_____
_____
_____
_____
_____
_____
_____
_____
_____
_____
_____

My Daily Plan

Date:_____

To-Do

Meal Plan

Breakfast:

Lunch:

Dinner:

Snacks:

Exercise & Water

Workout:

Water Goal:

Actual:

Notes

Schedule

5am_____
6am_____
7am_____
8am_____
9am_____
10am_____
11am_____
12pm_____
1pm_____
2pm_____
3pm_____
4pm_____
5pm_____
6pm_____
7pm_____
8pm_____

Other

Morning & Evening Reflection

Inspirational Quote / Memory Verse

What I'm Grateful For Today

Top Life Goals

Top 90-Day Goals

Goal Setting Actions for Today

My Accomplishments of the Day

What I Need To Improve On Tomorrow

Journal of My Day

_____
_____
_____
_____
_____
_____
_____
_____
_____
_____

My Daily Plan

Date:_____

To-Do

Meal Plan

Breakfast:

Lunch:

Dinner:

Snacks:

Exercise & Water

Workout:

Water Goal:

Actual:

Notes

Schedule

5am_____
6am_____
7am_____
8am_____
9am_____
10am_____
11am_____
12pm_____
1pm_____
2pm_____
3pm_____
4pm_____
5pm_____
6pm_____
7pm_____
8pm_____

Other

Morning & Evening Reflection

Inspirational Quote / Memory Verse

What I'm Grateful For Today

Top Life Goals

Top 90-Day Goals

Goal Setting Actions for Today

My Accomplishments of the Day

What I Need To Improve On Tomorrow

Journal of My Day

_____
_____
_____
_____
_____
_____
_____
_____
_____
_____

My Daily Plan

Date:_____

To-Do

Meal Plan

Breakfast:

Lunch:

Dinner:

Snacks:

Exercise & Water

Workout:

Water Goal:

Actual:

Notes

Schedule

5am_____
6am_____
7am_____
8am_____
9am_____
10am_____
11am_____
12pm_____
1pm_____
2pm_____
3pm_____
4pm_____
5pm_____
6pm_____
7pm_____
8pm_____

Other

Morning & Evening Reflection

Inspirational Quote / Memory Verse

What I'm Grateful For Today

Top Life Goals

Top 90-Day Goals

Goal Setting Actions for Today

My Accomplishments of the Day

What I Need To Improve On Tomorrow

Journal of My Day

_____
_____
_____
_____
_____
_____
_____
_____
_____
_____

My Daily Plan

Date:_____

To-Do

Meal Plan

Breakfast:

Lunch:

Dinner:

Snacks:

Exercise & Water

Workout:

Water Goal:

Actual:

Notes

Schedule

5am_____
6am_____
7am_____
8am_____
9am_____
10am_____
11am_____
12pm_____
1pm_____
2pm_____
3pm_____
4pm_____
5pm_____
6pm_____
7pm_____
8pm_____

Other

Morning & Evening Reflection

Inspirational Quote / Memory Verse

What I'm Grateful For Today

Top Life Goals

Top 90-Day Goals

Goal Setting Actions for Today

My Accomplishments of the Day

What I Need To Improve On Tomorrow

Journal of My Day

_____
_____
_____
_____
_____
_____
_____
_____
_____

My Daily Plan

Date:_____

To-Do

Meal Plan

Breakfast:

Lunch:

Dinner:

Snacks:

Exercise & Water

Workout:

Water Goal:

Actual:

Notes

Schedule

5am_____
6am_____
7am_____
8am_____
9am_____
10am_____
11am_____
12pm_____
1pm_____
2pm_____
3pm_____
4pm_____
5pm_____
6pm_____
7pm_____
8pm_____

Other

Morning & Evening Reflection

Inspirational Quote / Memory Verse

What I'm Grateful For Today

Top Life Goals

Top 90-Day Goals

Goal Setting Actions for Today

My Accomplishments of the Day

What I Need To Improve On Tomorrow

Journal of My Day

_____
_____
_____
_____
_____
_____
_____
_____
_____
_____

My Daily Plan

Date:_____

To-Do

Meal Plan

Breakfast:

Lunch:

Dinner:

Snacks:

Exercise & Water

Workout:

Water Goal:

Actual:

Notes

Schedule

5am_____
6am_____
7am_____
8am_____
9am_____
10am_____
11am_____
12pm_____
1pm_____
2pm_____
3pm_____
4pm_____
5pm_____
6pm_____
7pm_____
8pm_____

Other

Morning & Evening Reflection

Inspirational Quote / Memory Verse

What I'm Grateful For Today

Top Life Goals

Top 90-Day Goals

Goal Setting Actions for Today

My Accomplishments of the Day

What I Need To Improve On Tomorrow

Journal of My Day

_____
_____
_____
_____
_____
_____
_____
_____
_____
_____

My Daily Plan

Date:_____

To-Do

Meal Plan

Breakfast:

Lunch:

Dinner:

Snacks:

Exercise & Water

Workout:

Water Goal:

Actual:

Notes

Schedule

5am_____
6am_____
7am_____
8am_____
9am_____
10am_____
11am_____
12pm_____
1pm_____
2pm_____
3pm_____
4pm_____
5pm_____
6pm_____
7pm_____
8pm_____

Other

Morning & Evening Reflection

Inspirational Quote / Memory Verse

What I'm Grateful For Today

Top Life Goals

Top 90-Day Goals

Goal Setting Actions for Today

My Accomplishments of the Day

What I Need To Improve On Tomorrow

Journal of My Day

_____
_____
_____
_____
_____
_____
_____
_____
_____
_____

My Daily Plan

Date:_____

To-Do

Meal Plan

Breakfast:

Lunch:

Dinner:

Snacks:

Exercise & Water

Workout:

Water Goal:

Actual:

Notes

Schedule

5am_____
6am_____
7am_____
8am_____
9am_____
10am_____
11am_____
12pm_____
1pm_____
2pm_____
3pm_____
4pm_____
5pm_____
6pm_____
7pm_____
8pm_____

Other

Morning & Evening Reflection

Inspirational Quote / Memory Verse

What I'm Grateful For Today

Top Life Goals

Top 90-Day Goals

Goal Setting Actions for Today

My Accomplishments of the Day

What I Need To Improve On Tomorrow

Journal of My Day

_____
_____
_____
_____
_____
_____
_____
_____
_____
_____

My Daily Plan

Date:_____

To-Do

Meal Plan

Breakfast:

Lunch:

Dinner:

Snacks:

Exercise & Water

Workout:

Water Goal:

Actual:

Notes

Schedule

5am_____
6am_____
7am_____
8am_____
9am_____
10am_____
11am_____
12pm_____
1pm_____
2pm_____
3pm_____
4pm_____
5pm_____
6pm_____
7pm_____
8pm_____

Other

Morning & Evening Reflection

Inspirational Quote / Memory Verse

What I'm Grateful For Today

Top Life Goals

Top 90-Day Goals

Goal Setting Actions for Today

My Accomplishments of the Day

What I Need To Improve On Tomorrow

Journal of My Day

_____
_____
_____
_____
_____
_____
_____
_____
_____

My Daily Plan

Date:_____

To-Do

Meal Plan

Breakfast:

Lunch:

Dinner:

Snacks:

Exercise & Water

Workout:

Water Goal:

Actual:

Notes

Schedule

5am_____
6am_____
7am_____
8am_____
9am_____
10am_____
11am_____
12pm_____
1pm_____
2pm_____
3pm_____
4pm_____
5pm_____
6pm_____
7pm_____
8pm_____

Other

Morning & Evening Reflection

Inspirational Quote / Memory Verse

What I'm Grateful For Today

Top Life Goals

Top 90-Day Goals

Goal Setting Actions for Today

My Accomplishments of the Day

What I Need To Improve On Tomorrow

Journal of My Day

_____
_____
_____
_____
_____
_____
_____
_____
_____
_____

My Daily Plan

Date:_____

To-Do

Meal Plan

Breakfast:

Lunch:

Dinner:

Snacks:

Exercise & Water

Workout:

Water Goal:

Actual:

Notes

Schedule

5am_____
6am_____
7am_____
8am_____
9am_____
10am_____
11am_____
12pm_____
1pm_____
2pm_____
3pm_____
4pm_____
5pm_____
6pm_____
7pm_____
8pm_____

Other

Morning & Evening Reflection

Inspirational Quote / Memory Verse

What I'm Grateful For Today

Top Life Goals

Top 90-Day Goals

Goal Setting Actions for Today

My Accomplishments of the Day

What I Need To Improve On Tomorrow

Journal of My Day

___
___
___
___
___
___
___
___
___
___

My Daily Plan

Date:_____

To-Do

Meal Plan

Breakfast:

Lunch:

Dinner:

Snacks:

Exercise & Water

Workout:

Water Goal:

Actual:

Notes

Schedule

5am_____
6am_____
7am_____
8am_____
9am_____
10am_____
11am_____
12pm_____
1pm_____
2pm_____
3pm_____
4pm_____
5pm_____
6pm_____
7pm_____
8pm_____

Other

Morning & Evening Reflection

Inspirational Quote / Memory Verse

What I'm Grateful For Today

Top Life Goals

Top 90-Day Goals

Goal Setting Actions for Today

My Accomplishments of the Day

What I Need To Improve On Tomorrow

Journal of My Day

_____
_____
_____
_____
_____
_____
_____
_____
_____
_____

My Daily Plan

Date:_____

To-Do

Meal Plan

Breakfast:

Lunch:

Dinner:

Snacks:

Exercise & Water

Workout:

Water Goal:

Actual:

Notes

Schedule

5am_____
6am_____
7am_____
8am_____
9am_____
10am_____
11am_____
12pm_____
1pm_____
2pm_____
3pm_____
4pm_____
5pm_____
6pm_____
7pm_____
8pm_____

Other

Morning & Evening Reflection

Inspirational Quote / Memory Verse   **What I'm Grateful For Today**

Top Life Goals   Top 90-Day Goals

Goal Setting Actions for Today

My Accomplishments of the Day   What I Need To Improve On Tomorrow

Journal of My Day

_____
_____
_____
_____
_____
_____
_____
_____
_____

My Daily Plan

Date:_____

To-Do

Meal Plan

Breakfast:

Lunch:

Dinner:

Snacks:

Exercise & Water

Workout:

Water Goal:

Actual:

Notes

Schedule

5am_____
6am_____
7am_____
8am_____
9am_____
10am_____
11am_____
12pm_____
1pm_____
2pm_____
3pm_____
4pm_____
5pm_____
6pm_____
7pm_____
8pm_____

Other

Morning & Evening Reflection

Inspirational Quote / Memory Verse

What I'm Grateful For Today

Top Life Goals

Top 90-Day Goals

Goal Setting Actions for Today

My Accomplishments of the Day

What I Need To Improve On Tomorrow

Journal of My Day

_____
_____
_____
_____
_____
_____
_____
_____
_____
_____

My Daily Plan

Date:_____

To-Do

Meal Plan

Breakfast:

Lunch:

Dinner:

Snacks:

Exercise & Water

Workout:

Water Goal:

Actual:

Notes

Schedule

5am_____
6am_____
7am_____
8am_____
9am_____
10am_____
11am_____
12pm_____
1pm_____
2pm_____
3pm_____
4pm_____
5pm_____
6pm_____
7pm_____
8pm_____

Other

Morning & Evening Reflection

Inspirational Quote / Memory Verse   **What I'm Grateful For Today**

Top Life Goals   **Top 90-Day Goals**

Goal Setting Actions for Today

My Accomplishments of the Day   **What I Need To Improve On Tomorrow**

Journal of My Day

_____
_____
_____
_____
_____
_____
_____
_____
_____
_____

My Daily Plan

Date:_____

To-Do

Meal Plan

Breakfast:

Lunch:

Dinner:

Snacks:

Exercise & Water

Workout:

Water Goal:

Actual:

Notes

Schedule

5am_____
6am_____
7am_____
8am_____
9am_____
10am_____
11am_____
12pm_____
1pm_____
2pm_____
3pm_____
4pm_____
5pm_____
6pm_____
7pm_____
8pm_____

Other

Morning & Evening Reflection

Inspirational Quote / Memory Verse

What I'm Grateful For Today

Top Life Goals

Top 90-Day Goals

Goal Setting Actions for Today

My Accomplishments of the Day

What I Need To Improve On Tomorrow

Journal of My Day

_____
_____
_____
_____
_____
_____
_____
_____
_____
_____

My Daily Plan

Date:_____

To-Do

Meal Plan

Breakfast:

Lunch:

Dinner:

Snacks:

Exercise & Water

Workout:

Water Goal:

Actual:

Notes

Schedule

5am_____
6am_____
7am_____
8am_____
9am_____
10am_____
11am_____
12pm_____
1pm_____
2pm_____
3pm_____
4pm_____
5pm_____
6pm_____
7pm_____
8pm_____

Other

Morning & Evening Reflection

Inspirational Quote / Memory Verse

What I'm Grateful For Today

Top Life Goals

Top 90-Day Goals

Goal Setting Actions for Today

My Accomplishments of the Day

What I Need To Improve On Tomorrow

Journal of My Day

_____
_____
_____
_____
_____
_____
_____
_____
_____
_____

My Daily Plan

Date:_____

To-Do

Meal Plan

Breakfast:

Lunch:

Dinner:

Snacks:

Exercise & Water

Workout:

Water Goal:

Actual:

Notes

Schedule

5am_____
6am_____
7am_____
8am_____
9am_____
10am_____
11am_____
12pm_____
1pm_____
2pm_____
3pm_____
4pm_____
5pm_____
6pm_____
7pm_____
8pm_____

Other

Morning & Evening Reflection

Inspirational Quote / Memory Verse

What I'm Grateful For Today

Top Life Goals

Top 90-Day Goals

Goal Setting Actions for Today

My Accomplishments of the Day

What I Need To Improve On Tomorrow

Journal of My Day

_____
_____
_____
_____
_____
_____
_____
_____
_____
_____

My Daily Plan

Date:_____

To-Do

Meal Plan

Breakfast:

Lunch:

Dinner:

Snacks:

Exercise & Water

Workout:

Water Goal:

Actual:

Notes

Schedule

5am_____
6am_____
7am_____
8am_____
9am_____
10am_____
11am_____
12pm_____
1pm_____
2pm_____
3pm_____
4pm_____
5pm_____
6pm_____
7pm_____
8pm_____

Other

Morning & Evening Reflection

Inspirational Quote / Memory Verse

What I'm Grateful For Today

Top Life Goals

Top 90-Day Goals

Goal Setting Actions for Today

My Accomplishments of the Day

What I Need To Improve On Tomorrow

Journal of My Day

_____
_____
_____
_____
_____
_____
_____
_____
_____

My Daily Plan

Date:_____

To-Do

Meal Plan

Breakfast:

Lunch:

Dinner:

Snacks:

Exercise & Water

Workout:

Water Goal:

Actual:

Notes

Schedule

5am_____
6am_____
7am_____
8am_____
9am_____
10am_____
11am_____
12pm_____
1pm_____
2pm_____
3pm_____
4pm_____
5pm_____
6pm_____
7pm_____
8pm_____

Other

Morning & Evening Reflection

Inspirational Quote / Memory Verse

What I'm Grateful For Today

Top Life Goals

Top 90-Day Goals

Goal Setting Actions for Today

My Accomplishments of the Day

What I Need To Improve On Tomorrow

Journal of My Day

_____
_____
_____
_____
_____
_____
_____
_____
_____
_____

My Daily Plan

Date:_____

To-Do

Meal Plan

Breakfast:

Lunch:

Dinner:

Snacks:

Exercise & Water

Workout:

Water Goal:

Actual:

Notes

Schedule

5am_____
6am_____
7am_____
8am_____
9am_____
10am_____
11am_____
12pm_____
1pm_____
2pm_____
3pm_____
4pm_____
5pm_____
6pm_____
7pm_____
8pm_____

Other

Morning & Evening Reflection

Inspirational Quote / Memory Verse

What I'm Grateful For Today

Top Life Goals

Top 90-Day Goals

Goal Setting Actions for Today

My Accomplishments of the Day

What I Need To Improve On Tomorrow

Journal of My Day

_____
_____
_____
_____
_____
_____
_____
_____
_____
_____

My Daily Plan

Date:_____

To-Do

Meal Plan

Breakfast:

Lunch:

Dinner:

Snacks:

Exercise & Water

Workout:

Water Goal:

Actual:

Notes

Schedule

5am_____
6am_____
7am_____
8am_____
9am_____
10am_____
11am_____
12pm_____
1pm_____
2pm_____
3pm_____
4pm_____
5pm_____
6pm_____
7pm_____
8pm_____

Other

Morning & Evening Reflection

Inspirational Quote / Memory Verse   **What I'm Grateful For Today**

Top Life Goals   **Top 90-Day Goals**

Goal Setting Actions for Today

My Accomplishments of the Day   **What I Need To Improve On Tomorrow**

Journal of My Day

_____
_____
_____
_____
_____
_____
_____
_____
_____
_____

My Daily Plan

Date:_____

To-Do

Meal Plan

Breakfast:

Lunch:

Dinner:

Snacks:

Exercise & Water

Workout:

Water Goal:

Actual:

Notes

Schedule

5am_____
6am_____
7am_____
8am_____
9am_____
10am_____
11am_____
12pm_____
1pm_____
2pm_____
3pm_____
4pm_____
5pm_____
6pm_____
7pm_____
8pm_____

Other

Morning & Evening Reflection

Inspirational Quote / Memory Verse

What I'm Grateful For Today

Top Life Goals

Top 90-Day Goals

Goal Setting Actions for Today

My Accomplishments of the Day

What I Need To Improve On Tomorrow

Journal of My Day

_____
_____
_____
_____
_____
_____
_____
_____
_____
_____

My Daily Plan

Date:_____

To-Do

Meal Plan

Breakfast:

Lunch:

Dinner:

Snacks:

Exercise & Water

Workout:

Water Goal:

Actual:

Notes

Schedule

5am_____
6am_____
7am_____
8am_____
9am_____
10am_____
11am_____
12pm_____
1pm_____
2pm_____
3pm_____
4pm_____
5pm_____
6pm_____
7pm_____
8pm_____

Other

Morning & Evening Reflection

Inspirational Quote / Memory Verse

What I'm Grateful For Today

Top Life Goals

Top 90-Day Goals

Goal Setting Actions for Today

My Accomplishments of the Day

What I Need To Improve On Tomorrow

Journal of My Day

_____
_____
_____
_____
_____
_____
_____
_____
_____
_____

My Daily Plan

Date:_____

To-Do

Meal Plan

Breakfast:

Lunch:

Dinner:

Snacks:

Exercise & Water

Workout:

Water Goal:

Actual:

Notes

Schedule

5am_____
6am_____
7am_____
8am_____
9am_____
10am_____
11am_____
12pm_____
1pm_____
2pm_____
3pm_____
4pm_____
5pm_____
6pm_____
7pm_____
8pm_____

Other

Morning & Evening Reflection

Inspirational Quote / Memory Verse

What I'm Grateful For Today

Top Life Goals

Top 90-Day Goals

Goal Setting Actions for Today

My Accomplishments of the Day

What I Need To Improve On Tomorrow

Journal of My Day

_____
_____
_____
_____
_____
_____
_____
_____
_____
_____

My Daily Plan

Date:_____

To-Do

Meal Plan

Breakfast:

Lunch:

Dinner:

Snacks:

Exercise & Water

Workout:

Water Goal:

Actual:

Notes

Schedule

5am_____
6am_____
7am_____
8am_____
9am_____
10am_____
11am_____
12pm_____
1pm_____
2pm_____
3pm_____
4pm_____
5pm_____
6pm_____
7pm_____
8pm_____

Other

Morning & Evening Reflection

Inspirational Quote / Memory Verse

What I'm Grateful For Today

Top Life Goals

Top 90-Day Goals

Goal Setting Actions for Today

My Accomplishments of the Day

What I Need To Improve On Tomorrow

Journal of My Day

_____
_____
_____
_____
_____
_____
_____
_____
_____

My Daily Plan

Date:_____

To-Do

Meal Plan

Breakfast:

Lunch:

Dinner:

Snacks:

Exercise & Water

Workout:

Water Goal:

Actual:

Notes

Schedule

5am_____
6am_____
7am_____
8am_____
9am_____
10am_____
11am_____
12pm_____
1pm_____
2pm_____
3pm_____
4pm_____
5pm_____
6pm_____
7pm_____
8pm_____

Other

Morning & Evening Reflection

Inspirational Quote / Memory Verse

What I'm Grateful For Today

Top Life Goals

Top 90-Day Goals

Goal Setting Actions for Today

My Accomplishments of the Day

What I Need To Improve On Tomorrow

Journal of My Day

_____
_____
_____
_____
_____
_____
_____
_____
_____
_____
_____

My Daily Plan

Date:_____

To-Do

Meal Plan

Breakfast:

Lunch:

Dinner:

Snacks:

Exercise & Water

Workout:

Water Goal:

Actual:

Notes

Schedule

5am_____
6am_____
7am_____
8am_____
9am_____
10am_____
11am_____
12pm_____
1pm_____
2pm_____
3pm_____
4pm_____
5pm_____
6pm_____
7pm_____
8pm_____

Other

Morning & Evening Reflection

Inspirational Quote / Memory Verse

What I'm Grateful For Today

Top Life Goals

Top 90-Day Goals

Goal Setting Actions for Today

My Accomplishments of the Day

What I Need To Improve On Tomorrow

Journal of My Day

_____
_____
_____
_____
_____
_____
_____
_____
_____

My Daily Plan

Date:_____

To-Do

Meal Plan

Breakfast:

Lunch:

Dinner:

Snacks:

Exercise & Water

Workout:

Water Goal:

Actual:

Notes

Schedule

5am_____
6am_____
7am_____
8am_____
9am_____
10am_____
11am_____
12pm_____
1pm_____
2pm_____
3pm_____
4pm_____
5pm_____
6pm_____
7pm_____
8pm_____

Other

Morning & Evening Reflection

Inspirational Quote / Memory Verse

What I'm Grateful For Today

Top Life Goals

Top 90-Day Goals

Goal Setting Actions for Today

My Accomplishments of the Day

What I Need To Improve On Tomorrow

Journal of My Day

_____
_____
_____
_____
_____
_____
_____
_____
_____
_____

My Daily Plan

Date:_____

To-Do

Meal Plan

Breakfast:

Lunch:

Dinner:

Snacks:

Exercise & Water

Workout:

Water Goal:

Actual:

Notes

Schedule

5am_____
6am_____
7am_____
8am_____
9am_____
10am_____
11am_____
12pm_____
1pm_____
2pm_____
3pm_____
4pm_____
5pm_____
6pm_____
7pm_____
8pm_____

Other

Morning & Evening Reflection

Inspirational Quote / Memory Verse

What I'm Grateful For Today

Top Life Goals

Top 90-Day Goals

Goal Setting Actions for Today

My Accomplishments of the Day

What I Need To Improve On Tomorrow

Journal of My Day

_____
_____
_____
_____
_____
_____
_____
_____
_____
_____

My Daily Plan

Date:_____

To-Do

Meal Plan

Breakfast:

Lunch:

Dinner:

Snacks:

Exercise & Water

Workout:

Water Goal:

Actual:

Notes

Schedule

5am_____
6am_____
7am_____
8am_____
9am_____
10am_____
11am_____
12pm_____
1pm_____
2pm_____
3pm_____
4pm_____
5pm_____
6pm_____
7pm_____
8pm_____

Other

Morning & Evening Reflection

Inspirational Quote / Memory Verse

What I'm Grateful For Today

Top Life Goals

Top 90-Day Goals

Goal Setting Actions for Today

My Accomplishments of the Day

What I Need To Improve On Tomorrow

Journal of My Day

_____
_____
_____
_____
_____
_____
_____
_____
_____
_____

My Daily Plan

Date:_____

To-Do

Meal Plan

Breakfast:

Lunch:

Dinner:

Snacks:

Exercise & Water

Workout:

Water Goal:

Actual:

Notes

Schedule

5am_____
6am_____
7am_____
8am_____
9am_____
10am_____
11am_____
12pm_____
1pm_____
2pm_____
3pm_____
4pm_____
5pm_____
6pm_____
7pm_____
8pm_____

Other

Morning & Evening Reflection

Inspirational Quote / Memory Verse

What I'm Grateful For Today

Top Life Goals

Top 90-Day Goals

Goal Setting Actions for Today

My Accomplishments of the Day

What I Need To Improve On Tomorrow

Journal of My Day

_____
_____
_____
_____
_____
_____
_____
_____
_____
_____

My Daily Plan

Date:_____

To-Do

Meal Plan

Breakfast:

Lunch:

Dinner:

Snacks:

Exercise & Water

Workout:

Water Goal:

Actual:

Notes

Schedule

5am_____
6am_____
7am_____
8am_____
9am_____
10am_____
11am_____
12pm_____
1pm_____
2pm_____
3pm_____
4pm_____
5pm_____
6pm_____
7pm_____
8pm_____

Other

Morning & Evening Reflection

Inspirational Quote / Memory Verse

What I'm Grateful For Today

Top Life Goals

Top 90-Day Goals

Goal Setting Actions for Today

My Accomplishments of the Day

What I Need To Improve On Tomorrow

Journal of My Day

_____
_____
_____
_____
_____
_____
_____
_____
_____
_____

My Daily Plan

Date:_____

To-Do

Meal Plan

Breakfast:

Lunch:

Dinner:

Snacks:

Exercise & Water

Workout:

Water Goal:

Actual:

Notes

Schedule

5am_____
6am_____
7am_____
8am_____
9am_____
10am_____
11am_____
12pm_____
1pm_____
2pm_____
3pm_____
4pm_____
5pm_____
6pm_____
7pm_____
8pm_____

Other

Morning & Evening Reflection

Inspirational Quote / Memory Verse

What I'm Grateful For Today

Top Life Goals

Top 90-Day Goals

Goal Setting Actions for Today

My Accomplishments of the Day

What I Need To Improve On Tomorrow

Journal of My Day

_____
_____
_____
_____
_____
_____
_____
_____
_____
_____

My Daily Plan

Date:_____

To-Do

Meal Plan

Breakfast:

Lunch:

Dinner:

Snacks:

Exercise & Water

Workout:

Water Goal:

Actual:

Notes

Schedule

5am_____
6am_____
7am_____
8am_____
9am_____
10am_____
11am_____
12pm_____
1pm_____
2pm_____
3pm_____
4pm_____
5pm_____
6pm_____
7pm_____
8pm_____

Other

Morning & Evening Reflection

Inspirational Quote / Memory Verse

What I'm Grateful For Today

Top Life Goals

Top 90-Day Goals

Goal Setting Actions for Today

My Accomplishments of the Day

What I Need To Improve On Tomorrow

Journal of My Day

_____
_____
_____
_____
_____
_____
_____
_____
_____
_____

My Daily Plan

Date:_____

To-Do

Meal Plan

Breakfast:

Lunch:

Dinner:

Snacks:

Exercise & Water

Workout:

Water Goal:

Actual:

Notes

Schedule

5am_____
6am_____
7am_____
8am_____
9am_____
10am_____
11am_____
12pm_____
1pm_____
2pm_____
3pm_____
4pm_____
5pm_____
6pm_____
7pm_____
8pm_____

Other

Morning & Evening Reflection

Inspirational Quote / Memory Verse

What I'm Grateful For Today

Top Life Goals

Top 90-Day Goals

Goal Setting Actions for Today

My Accomplishments of the Day

What I Need To Improve On Tomorrow

Journal of My Day

_____
_____
_____
_____
_____
_____
_____
_____
_____
_____

My Daily Plan

Date:_____

To-Do

Meal Plan

Breakfast:

Lunch:

Dinner:

Snacks:

Exercise & Water

Workout:

Water Goal:

Actual:

Notes

Schedule

5am_____
6am_____
7am_____
8am_____
9am_____
10am_____
11am_____
12pm_____
1pm_____
2pm_____
3pm_____
4pm_____
5pm_____
6pm_____
7pm_____
8pm_____

Other

Morning & Evening Reflection

Inspirational Quote / Memory Verse

What I'm Grateful For Today

Top Life Goals

Top 90-Day Goals

Goal Setting Actions for Today

My Accomplishments of the Day

What I Need To Improve On Tomorrow

Journal of My Day

_____
_____
_____
_____
_____
_____
_____
_____
_____
_____

My Daily Plan

Date:_____

To-Do

Meal Plan

Breakfast:

Lunch:

Dinner:

Snacks:

Exercise & Water

Workout:

Water Goal:

Actual:

Notes

Schedule

5am_____
6am_____
7am_____
8am_____
9am_____
10am_____
11am_____
12pm_____
1pm_____
2pm_____
3pm_____
4pm_____
5pm_____
6pm_____
7pm_____
8pm_____

Other

Morning & Evening Reflection

Inspirational Quote / Memory Verse

What I'm Grateful For Today

Top Life Goals

Top 90-Day Goals

Goal Setting Actions for Today

My Accomplishments of the Day

What I Need To Improve On Tomorrow

Journal of My Day

_____
_____
_____
_____
_____
_____
_____
_____
_____
_____

My Daily Plan

Date:_____

To-Do

Meal Plan

Breakfast:

Lunch:

Dinner:

Snacks:

Exercise & Water

Workout:

Water Goal:

Actual:

Notes

Schedule

5am_____
6am_____
7am_____
8am_____
9am_____
10am_____
11am_____
12pm_____
1pm_____
2pm_____
3pm_____
4pm_____
5pm_____
6pm_____
7pm_____
8pm_____

Other

Morning & Evening Reflection

Inspirational Quote / Memory Verse

What I'm Grateful For Today

Top Life Goals

Top 90-Day Goals

Goal Setting Actions for Today

My Accomplishments of the Day

What I Need To Improve On Tomorrow

Journal of My Day

_____
_____
_____
_____
_____
_____
_____
_____
_____
_____
_____

My Daily Plan

Date:_____

To-Do

Meal Plan

Breakfast:

Lunch:

Dinner:

Snacks:

Exercise & Water

Workout:

Water Goal:

Actual:

Notes

Schedule

5am_____
6am_____
7am_____
8am_____
9am_____
10am_____
11am_____
12pm_____
1pm_____
2pm_____
3pm_____
4pm_____
5pm_____
6pm_____
7pm_____
8pm_____

Other

Morning & Evening Reflection

Inspirational Quote / Memory Verse

What I'm Grateful For Today

Top Life Goals

Top 90-Day Goals

Goal Setting Actions for Today

My Accomplishments of the Day

What I Need To Improve On Tomorrow

Journal of My Day

_____
_____
_____
_____
_____
_____
_____
_____
_____
_____

My Daily Plan

Date:_____

To-Do

Meal Plan

Breakfast:

Lunch:

Dinner:

Snacks:

Exercise & Water

Workout:

Water Goal:

Actual:

Notes

Schedule

5am_____
6am_____
7am_____
8am_____
9am_____
10am_____
11am_____
12pm_____
1pm_____
2pm_____
3pm_____
4pm_____
5pm_____
6pm_____
7pm_____
8pm_____

Other

Morning & Evening Reflection

Inspirational Quote / Memory Verse

What I'm Grateful For Today

Top Life Goals

Top 90-Day Goals

Goal Setting Actions for Today

My Accomplishments of the Day

What I Need To Improve On Tomorrow

Journal of My Day

_____
_____
_____
_____
_____
_____
_____
_____
_____
_____

My Daily Plan

Date:_____

To-Do

Meal Plan

Breakfast:

Lunch:

Dinner:

Snacks:

Exercise & Water

Workout:

Water Goal:

Actual:

Notes

Schedule

5am_____
6am_____
7am_____
8am_____
9am_____
10am_____
11am_____
12pm_____
1pm_____
2pm_____
3pm_____
4pm_____
5pm_____
6pm_____
7pm_____
8pm_____

Other

Morning & Evening Reflection

Inspirational Quote / Memory Verse

What I'm Grateful For Today

Top Life Goals

Top 90-Day Goals

Goal Setting Actions for Today

My Accomplishments of the Day

What I Need To Improve On Tomorrow

Journal of My Day

_____
_____
_____
_____
_____
_____
_____
_____
_____
_____

My Daily Plan

Date:_____

To-Do

Meal Plan

Breakfast:

Lunch:

Dinner:

Snacks:

Exercise & Water

Workout:

Water Goal:

Actual:

Notes

Schedule

5am_____
6am_____
7am_____
8am_____
9am_____
10am_____
11am_____
12pm_____
1pm_____
2pm_____
3pm_____
4pm_____
5pm_____
6pm_____
7pm_____
8pm_____

Other

Morning & Evening Reflection

Inspirational Quote / Memory Verse

What I'm Grateful For Today

Top Life Goals

Top 90-Day Goals

Goal Setting Actions for Today

My Accomplishments of the Day

What I Need To Improve On Tomorrow

Journal of My Day

_____
_____
_____
_____
_____
_____
_____
_____
_____

~A 90-Day Review~

Date:_____

My 90-Day Wins:

_____
_____
_____
_____
_____
_____
_____
_____
_____
_____

What habits or actions can I improve on in my next 90-Day Cycle?

_____
_____
_____
_____
_____
_____
_____
_____
_____
_____
_____
_____

What I have learned:

_____
_____
_____
_____
_____
_____
_____
_____
_____
_____

What I am grateful for:

_____
_____
_____
_____
_____
_____
_____
_____
_____
_____
_____

Notes

Notes

Notes

Notes

Notes

Notes

Notes

Notes